CHEMICALS IN ACTION

ATOMS

Chris Oxlade

REVISED AND UPDATED

Heinemann Library

Chicago, Illinois

© 2002, 2007 Heinemann Library
a division of Reed Elsevier Inc.
Chicago, Illinois

Customer Service 888-454-2279
Visit our website at www.heinemannraintree.com

Editorial: Clare Lewis
Design: Steve Mead and Fiona MacColl
Picture Research: Hannah Taylor
Production: Julie Carter
Originated by Modern Age
Printed and bound in China by Leo Paper Group

11 10 09 08 07
10 9 8 7 6 5 4 3 2 1

New edition ISBN: 978-1-4329-0051-9 (hardcover)
                  978-1-4329-0058-8 (paperback)

The Library of Congress has cataloged the first edition as follows:
Oxlade, Chris
    Atoms / Chris Oxlade.
        p. cm. -- (Chemicals in action)
    Includes bibliographical references and index.
    ISBN 1-58810-195-9 (lib. bdg.)
    1. Atomic theory -- Juvenile literature. 2.
Matter--Constitution—Juvenile literature. [1. Atomic theory. 2.
Atoms. 3. Matter--Constitution.] I. Title.
QD461 .O95 2001
539.7—dc21
                                00-012488

Acknowledgments
The author and publishers are grateful to the following for permission to reproduce copyright material: Ace Photo Agency pp. **12**, **18**, Alamy pp. **37**, **38**, Andrew Lambert pp. **24**, **33** (top), Bridgeman Art Library p. **9**, Corbis p. **4**, Food Features p. **34**, Mary Evans Picture Library pp. **8**, **21**, Milepost 92 p. **32**, Oxford Scientific Films (David Macdonald) p. **35**, Science Photo Library pp. **5**, **6**, **7**, **10**, **11**, **16**, **19**, **22**, **25**, **26**, **36**, **39**, Trevor Clifford pp. **17**, **23**, **27**, **29**, **30**, **31**, **33** (bottom).

Cover photograph: computer artwork representing the structure of an atom, reproduced with permission of Science Photo Library/Michael Dunning.

The publishers would like to thank Ted Dolter and Dr. Nigel Saunders for their assistance in the preparation of this title.

Every effort has been made to contact copyright holders of any material reproduced in this book. Any omissions will be rectified in subsequent printings if notice is given to the publisher.

The paper used to print this book comes from sustainable sources.

Some words are shown in bold, **like this**. You can find out what they mean by looking in the glossary.

CONTENTS

CHEMICALS IN ACTION

What's the link between plastics, the **genes** that control our bodies, and nuclear weapons? The answer is **atoms**. They are all made of atoms or use atoms to work. In fact, almost every substance is made of atoms. Our knowledge of how atoms and other **particles** behave is used in making chemicals, in medical research, in power generation, and engineering.

The study of atoms is part of the science of chemistry. Many people think of chemistry as something that scientists study by doing experiments in laboratories with special equipment. This part of chemistry is very important. It is how scientists find out what substances are made of, and how they make new materials. But this is only a small part of chemistry. Most chemistry happens away from laboratories, in factories and chemical plants. It is used to manufacture a wide range of items, such as synthetic fibers for fabrics, drugs to treat diseases, explosives for fireworks, solvents for paints, and fertilizers for growing crops.

This is what happens when atoms split apart. A nuclear bomb test explosion in Nevada.

About the experiments and activities

There are several experiments and activities for you to try. They will help you understand some of the chemistry in the book. An experiment is designed to help solve a scientific problem. Scientists use a logical approach to experiments, so that they can make conclusions from the results of the experiments. A scientist first writes down a hypothesis, which he or she thinks might be the answer to the problem, then designs an experiment to test the hypothesis. He or she writes down the results of the experiment and concludes whether or not the results show that the hypothesis is true. We only know what we do about chemistry because scientists have carefully carried out thousands of experiments over hundreds of years. Experiments have allowed scientists to discover first that atoms exist, then what they are made of, and how they join together.

DOING THE EXPERIMENTS AND ACTIVITIES

All the experiments and activities in this book have been designed for you to do at home with everyday substances and equipment. They can also be done in your school's science class. Always follow the safety advice given with each experiment or activity. Ask an adult to help you when the instructions tell you to.

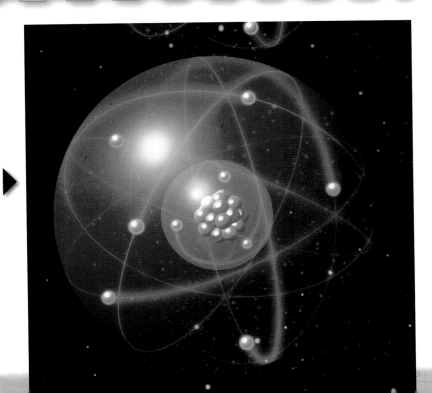

A model of an atom, made up of a nucleus with electrons around it. The actual atom is billions of times smaller.

ALL ABOUT ATOMS

Everything in your home or school (including you), everything on Earth, Earth itself, and everything else in the whole Universe, is made of **matter**. When scientists use the word "matter," they mean any substance that exists, from everyday substances such as wood, plastic, water, and the air that we breathe, to the stars and planets deep in space.

All matter is made up of extremely tiny particles called atoms. Imagine breaking up an object, such as a **metal** pin, into smaller and smaller pieces. If you kept breaking it up, eventually you would end up with just atoms of the metal, which you could not break up. Of course, this would be impossible in practice using everyday tools, because the pieces of metal would soon become far too small to break.

▲ Almost everything in the Universe, such as this enormous nebula (cloud of dust) and the stars that are being born in it, is made of atoms.

The size of atoms

Atoms are almost unimaginably small—the biggest ones are roughly a billionth of an inch across. If you were to write a period with a pencil, the period would contain millions and millions of carbon atoms from the graphite in the pencil. It also means that if you blew up those atoms until they were each an inch across, the period would be about 20 miles wide!

This tiny crystal, called a microcrystal, is made up of seven uranium atoms. The picture was taken with a scanning transmission electron microscope (STEM), which can magnify objects more than 90 million times.

Types of atom

There are many different types of atoms, and 90 different types have been found naturally occurring on Earth. They make up the rocks and soil in Earth's crust, the gases in the Earth's **atmosphere**, and the plants and animals that live on Earth. More types of atoms have been made by scientists in laboratories, often by smashing other atoms together at extremely high speed. Very special conditions are needed to create these atoms, and the atoms normally only exist for a fraction of a second before they disintegrate again.

Different substances look different and have different **properties**, such as different strengths and **boiling points**. This is because they are made up of different types of atoms joined together in different ways.

THEORIES ABOUT MATTER

Some of the first people who tried to explain the properties and behavior of matter were philosophers who lived in ancient Greece about 2,500 years ago. Their **theories** were really just guesses, often based on their religious beliefs, and they did not carry out experiments to test these theories. The philosophers were called natural philosophers. One of the most famous, Thales of Miletus, lived in the 6th century B.C. His theory was that all matter is made up of water.

Ideas about atoms

In 430 B.C. another philosopher, Democritus of Abdera, tried to explain why different substances have different properties, such as different strengths, colors, and tastes. His theory was that all matter is made up of tiny building blocks, and that these blocks cannot be divided into smaller pieces. He named the blocks *atomos*, which means "indivisible". This was the origin of the word atom that we use today. Democritus believed that in light substances, the blocks have big spaces between them, and that in heavy substances, the blocks are tightly packed together. He also believed that the properties of a substance are caused by the shape of the atoms in them. For example, he thought that things that tasted sour were made up of blocks with spikes on the outside!

Other Greek philosophers said that these ideas about atoms were nonsense. They agreed with another theory, that all matter was made from four basic elements – earth, fire, water, and air. This theory said that different substances contained different amounts of the four elements.

Greek philosopher
Democritus of Abdera

Eventually most philosophers accepted the idea about four basic elements, because two very important philosophers of the time, Aristotle and Plato, supported it. It is important to know that these philosophers did not do any experiments to test if their ideas were right or wrong. Their ideas were simply ideas, but they were still accepted 2,000 years later, in the 1600s.

Gold from lead

The chemists of the Middle Ages (which lasted from about the 400s to about the 1400s) were called alchemists. Alchemy was a strange mixture of science, magic, astrology, and religion. One of the things alchemists tried to do was to make gold and silver from other metals, such as lead and mercury. They did not succeed, but they did discover many new substances in the process.

The Alchemist's Workshop, painted in 1570, shows alchemists at work trying to make precious metals from everyday metals.

Experimental science

The earth, air, fire, and water idea of the Greek philosophers was accepted as the truth in Europe for many centuries. Things only began to change after the 1400s, when scientists started to carry out real scientific experiments.

One of the most important things that scientists needed to do was to find out what matter was made of. Gradually the scientists realized that the ancient Greek idea about the four elements was incorrect. Instead, the idea that matter is made of atoms became accepted by most scientists. Among them was Irish scientist Robert Boyle (1627–1691), who defined an **element**. He said that an element was a substance made up of atoms that cannot be broken into more simple substances. He suggested that most substances are not elements, but are made up of different elements combined together. He also said that atoms come in different shapes and sizes.

Robert Boyle (1627–1691) was one of the first scientists to do experiments in a logical way. He argued that chemists should not be trying to turn lead into gold, but should be figuring out what substances are made from.

Because these scientists used experiments to try to prove their theories, their work became known as experimental science. There was a rapid rise in experimental science in the 1700s and 1800s. The knowledge we have today about atoms, and how they combine to make different substances, was discovered during this time.

Dalton's atomic theory

One of the most important theories, called the **atomic theory**, came from John Dalton (see below). He decided that there are a limited number of types of atom, which combine together to form millions of different substances. Dalton stated that each element (such as carbon, oxygen, or iron) is made up of atoms; that all the atoms of an element are the same; and that atoms cannot be broken apart. Before this, many scientists believed that each and every different substance was made up of a different type of atom.

JOHN DALTON (1766–1844)

English scientist John Dalton lived in northern England. He was very intelligent and started working as a teacher at his local school when he was just 12 years old! He became a full-time scientist in his mid-30s. As well as chemistry, he studied color-blindness (from which he suffered) and the weather, which he recorded on nearly every day of his life. Some of Dalton's ideas were wrong and some of his experiments were inaccurate, but his atomic theory became the basis of modern theories about matter.

ATOMS AND ELEMENTS

Today scientists around the world agree that all substances are made up of atoms of one or more different elements—but what is the difference between an atom and an element?

An atom is an extremely tiny particle of matter, and there are more than a hundred different types of atoms. An element is a substance that contains only one type of atom. For example, iron is an element because it is made up of just iron atoms. Every atom in a piece of iron is exactly the same as all the others. Because an element is made up of just one type of atom, there is an element for each different type of atom. So there are the same number of elements as there are different types of atoms.

Metals and nonmetals

About three-quarters of the elements are metals, such as iron, aluminum, copper, silver, and gold. Metals are shiny, they are good conductors of heat and electricity, and they are usually solid at room temperature. The only exception is mercury, which is a liquid metal.

The rest of the elements are **nonmetals**, such as carbon, oxygen, hydrogen, nitrogen, and sulfur. Most nonmetals are poor conductors of heat and electricity. Most are gases at room temperature, a few are solids and only one, bromine, is a liquid.

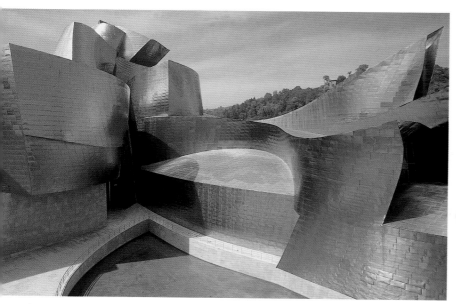

Some elements are called **metalloids** or semimetals. This is because they have some of the properties of metals, and some of the properties of nonmetals.

Spectacular metal protective coating on the Guggenheim Museum, Spain.

Names and symbols

Every element has a name, and scientists have also given each one a **symbol** that is used to represent the element in **chemical formulas** and equations. Each symbol is an abbreviation (a shortened version) of the element's name. For example, the chemical symbol for the element carbon is C. The symbols given to elements do not always seem to match their names. This is because the symbols come from different languages. For example, the symbol for iron is Fe, which comes from *ferrum*, the Latin word for iron.

Compounds and mixtures

All substances are either elements, **compounds**, or **mixtures**. An element is made up of only one type of atom. Carbon and oxygen are both elements. A compound is a substance made up of two or more elements joined together. For example, when carbon atoms join with oxygen atoms, they make a compound called carbon dioxide. Carbon atoms that are just mixed with oxygen atoms, but are not attached to them, form a mixture. A mixture can also contain compounds, as long as they are not joined to the other substances in the mixture. For example, air is a mixture of elements such as nitrogen and oxygen, and compounds, such as water and carbon dioxide.

This diagram shows the difference between two separate elements, a simple compound made up of the elements joined together, and a mixture of the two elements.

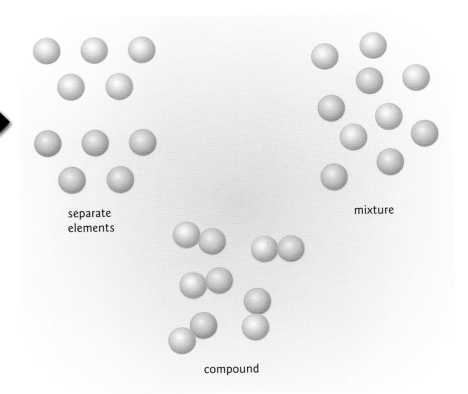

separate elements

mixture

compound

Inside atoms

Atoms themselves are extremely tiny, but they are made up of even tinier particles. These particles are impossible to see even with the most powerful microscopes, but they can be detected with sensitive scientific instruments. They are called **sub-atomic particles** because they are even smaller than an atom.

The nucleus

At the center of every atom is a **nucleus**. The nucleus is made up of particles called protons and neutrons, joined closely to each other in a bunch.

In most atoms there are about the same number of protons and neutrons in the nucleus. For example, the nucleus of a carbon atom contains six protons and six neutrons, and the nucleus of a lithium atom contains three protons and four neutrons. The simplest atoms are hydrogen atoms, because the nucleus is a single proton.

The nucleus of an atom is extremely small compared to the size of the atom itself. Imagine if an atom was blown up to the size of an Olympic running track, its nucleus would still only be the size of a pea!

At the center of ▶ every atom is a nucleus, made up of protons and neutrons. Electrons travel around the nucleus.

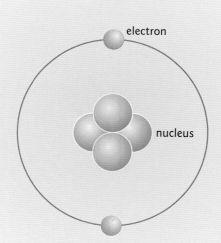

Bohr model of a helium atom

electron

nucleus

The protons and neutrons in the nucleus of an atom make up nearly all its weight, and protons and neutrons weigh the same as each other. Protons also have a tiny electric charge. This charge is similar to what you get on your hair when you comb it and it stands up on its own. There are two types of electric charge—positive and negative. Protons have a positive electric charge, neutrons have no electric charge.

Electrons

Particles called **electrons** travel around the nucleus. They are a fraction of the size and weight of protons and neutrons. A complete atom always has the same number of electrons as protons in the nucleus. Electrons have a negative electric charge, equal in size but opposite to the charge of a proton. In a complete atom, the negative charges of the electrons cancel out the positive charges of the protons, so overall there is no electric charge.

Atomic number and mass

The atoms of different elements have different numbers of protons, neutrons, and electrons. All the atoms of an element have the same number of protons. For example, all carbon atoms have six protons. The number of protons in an atom is called its atomic number, or sometimes its proton number. The atomic number of carbon is six, because its atoms all have six protons. If you add the number of protons in an atom to the number of neutrons in an atom, you get the atom's mass number. The mass number of a carbon atom with six protons and six neutrons is twelve.

This diagram shows how the number of protons and neutrons in an atom of carbon relate to its mass number and atomic number.

carbon atom nucleus

mass number = 12

protons — atomic number = 6

neutrons

Model atoms

You often see diagrams similar to the one on page 14 that show what an atom looks like, but atoms don't actually look like this! The drawings only show what scientists think the structure of an atom is like—they are models of atoms. Scientists have never actually seen an atom, because the sub-atomic particles are invisible. They only have evidence from experiments about what the structure is like, so the models are really still theories.

Scientists know that an atom has a nucleus at the center, and electrons around it, but they do not really know how the electrons move around the nucleus. In some atomic models, electrons are shown orbiting the nucleus, like the planets orbiting the Sun, and in other models they are shown moving around in groups.

DEVELOPING A MODEL ATOM

The modern model of the atom was developed by British physicist Ernest Rutherford (1871–1937) and Danish physicist Niels Bohr (1885–1962). In 1911 Rutherford carried out an experiment in which he fired sub-atomic particles at a sheet of material. He found that most went straight through, but a few bounced back. He concluded that atoms must be made up mostly of empty space, with their mass concentrated in a central nucleus. Most of the particles

simply went straight through the empty spaces in the sheet of material, and only a few hit the atoms' nuclei and bounced back. In 1913 Bohr (seen here) developed his atomic model that shows electrons orbiting the nucleus in different layers called **shells**.

EXPERIMENT: MAKING MODELS OF ATOMS

Here you can see how to make some simple models of atoms. They will help you understand and remember the structure of atoms.

EQUIPMENT
- modeling clay in three different colors

Activity steps

1 Make six balls about ½ inch (10 millimeters) across from one color of clay. These are your model protons. Make six more balls the same size, but in a different color. These are your model neutrons. Make six balls about ¼ inch (5 millimeters) across, but in a third color. These are your model electrons.

2 Hydrogen is the simplest atom. It only has one proton and one electron. Try making a model of a hydrogen atom. Put one proton on the table and put one electron near it, but not touching. If you wanted to make a scale model, the electron would have to be about a third of a mile (0.5 kilometers) away from the proton!

3 Try making a model helium atom (right). Make a nucleus by joining two protons and two neutrons into a bunch, and put two electrons in an imaginary circle around it. Remember not to let the electrons touch the nucleus or each other.

4 Try making a model carbon atom (carbon atoms have six protons, six neutrons, and six electrons). When you put the electrons around the nucleus, put two electrons close to the nucleus and the other four electrons farther away. This models two electron shells.

5 The number of protons is called the atomic number. What is the atomic number of carbon? The number of protons added to the number of neutrons is called the mass number. What is the mass number of carbon?

6 The proton number of beryllium is four and its mass number is nine. Try making a model beryllium atom.

Joining atoms

Objects like this book, your pen, and your whole body are made up of countless billions of atoms. These atoms must be joined together, or the objects would fall apart. But exactly how are atoms attached to each other? The answer is that they are joined together by links called **chemical bonds**.

Making atoms stable

As we have seen, electrons are arranged around the nucleus of an atom in layers called shells. The shells are like the layers of skin on an onion. Each layer can hold a certain number of electrons before it becomes full. When it is full, another layer is started. The more electrons an atom has, the more shells it needs to hold them all. See page 44 for some examples.

Stable or unreactive atoms have completely full outer shells. If an atom has an outer shell with only one or two electrons, it is unstable and **reactive**. It can become stable by losing its outer electrons. This empties the shell, and leaves the full shell underneath as the new outer shell. An atom is also unstable if it needs one or two electrons to fill its outer shell. In this case, it can become stable by gaining electrons from another atom to fill its outer shell. It can also become stable by sharing electrons with another atom.

Atoms that have only one or two electrons in their outer shell often give them away to become stable. For example, a sodium atom has only one electron in its outer shell. It always loses this electron to become stable. This leaves it with 11 positively **charged** protons but only 10 negatively charged electrons, so overall it has a single positive charge. The sodium atom has become a sodium **ion**, and its symbol is Na^+.

All the noble gases are unreactive. This blimp is full of helium, which would not explode in an accident.

Metallic bonds are generally very strong, which is why metals tend to have very high **melting points**. This steel is solid, even though it is red hot.

Atoms that need one or two electrons to give them a full outer shell often gain extra electrons from other atoms to become stable. For example, a chlorine atom has an outer shell that needs one more electron to make it full. So, a chlorine atom will gain one electron to become stable. This leaves it with 17 positively charged protons but 18 negatively charged electrons, so overall it has a single negative charge. The chlorine atom has become a chloride ion, and its symbol is Cl$^-$.

Atoms that have too few electrons to make a full shell can become stable by sharing electrons with each other. Two atoms can be so close together that they can share the electrons in their outer shells. If two electrons are shared, this makes a bond between the two atoms called a **covalent bond**. For example, a chlorine atom has 17 electrons, but needs 18 to have a full outer shell. If two chlorine atoms join together so that they share two electrons, one from each atom, each of them will have 18 electrons. They will be joined together by a covalent bond, and both atoms will be stable.

Metallic bonding

In a piece of metal, such as iron, the atoms become stable by sharing electrons. In metals, the electrons that are shared are not fixed in their shells, but can move from atom to atom. This does not make the atoms unstable, because overall each atom still has enough electrons. An electric current is made up of a stream of electrons, so metals are good conductors of electricity.

The periodic table

The periodic table is a list of all the known elements, arranged in order of the atomic numbers of their atoms, starting at the top left and working across and down. Elements with similar properties are close together. For example, fluorine (F) is a gas that reacts very easily with other elements and so is chlorine (Cl). The periodic table gets its name from the fact that the elements' properties repeat themselves every few elements, or periodically. A chemist can tell what the properties of an element are likely to be by looking at its position in the table.

Groups and periods

The vertical columns of elements are called groups. Elements in a group all have similar properties to each other. The horizontal rows of elements are called periods. The table also shows which elements are metals, which are nonmetals, and which are metalloids. Some groups have special names:

Group 1: The alkali metals
Group 2: The alkaline earth metals
Group 17: The halogens
Group 18: The noble gases

The periodic table, showing the position of each group (vertical block of elements). The full table is on pages 40–41.

Group 1	Group 2					
H						
Li	Be					
Na	Mg			Groups 3–12		
K	Ca					
Rb	Sr			Transition metals		
Cs	Ba					
Fr	Ra					

DMITRI MENDELEYEV (1834–1907)

The Russian scientist Dmitri Mendeleyev was born in Siberia and became a chemistry professor at St. Petersburg in 1866. In 1869 he drew up the first periodic table. Mendeleyev's clever idea was to leave spaces in the table where no known elements fitted neatly. He predicted that elements would soon be discovered to fill the gaps, and by 1950 all the spaces he left had been filled!

Group 13	Group 14	Group 15	Group 16	Group 17	Group 18
					He
B	C	N	O	F	Ne
Al	Si	P	S	Cl	Ar
Ga	Ge	As	Se	Br	Kr
In	Sn	Sb	Te	I	Xe
Tl	Pb	Bi	Po	At	Rn
Uut	Uuq	Uup	Uuh		

MOLECULES

All substances are made up of tiny particles. In some substances, the particles are individual atoms or ions, and in other substances, they are groups of atoms called **molecules**. A molecule is made up of two or more atoms joined together by covalent bonds. For example, a hydrogen molecule is made up of two hydrogen atoms joined together by one covalent bond; an oxygen molecule is made up of two oxygen atoms joined together by two covalent bonds.

A compound is a substance that contains two or more different elements. Many compounds are made up of molecules. For example, water is a compound of oxygen and hydrogen that is made up of molecules. Each and every water molecule contains one oxygen atom and two hydrogen atoms.

Symbols and formulas

Scientists need a clear way of showing what atoms are in the molecules of a substance. To do this they use chemical formulas. The formula tells you how many atoms of each element are in each of its molecules. For example, the formula of oxygen is O_2, which shows that each oxygen molecule contains two oxygen atoms. The formula for water is H_2O, which shows that each water molecule contains two atoms of hydrogen and one atom of oxygen.

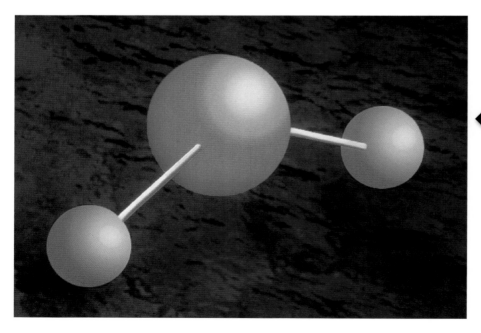

A model of a molecule of water. Each and every water molecule has an oxygen atom with two hydrogen atoms joined to it.

EXPERIMENT: MAKING MOLECULES

Problem   How do molecules of compounds form?

Hypothesis   Molecules of a compound contain atoms of different elements, and they could be formed when molecules of the elements react together.

EQUIPMENT
- modeling clay (two different colors)
- matchsticks or wooden dowels

Experiment steps

1 Make four balls about ½ inch (10 millimeters) across from one color of modeling clay. These are your model hydrogen atoms. Make two balls about 1 inch (20 millimeters) across and in a different color. These are your model oxygen atoms.

2 Make a model hydrogen molecule by joining two hydrogen atoms together with a matchstick. Make sure the atoms do not touch each other. The matchstick is the model bond between the two hydrogen atoms. Make one more hydrogen molecule.

3 Make a model oxygen molecule by joining two oxygen atoms using two matchsticks side by side (oxygen atoms can make two bonds each).

4 Now model the reaction between hydrogen and oxygen to make water. Take apart the model hydrogen molecules and oxygen molecule and join them together to make two water molecules (each water molecule is made of two hydrogen atoms joined to an oxygen atom). If you have done it correctly, you will still have the same number of atoms

This is the symbol equation for the reaction: $2H_2 + O_2 \rightarrow 2H_2O$

Simple molecules and giant molecules

The molecules of many substances, such as oxygen and water, are made up of a small number of atoms. Molecules like this are called simple molecules. The molecules of other substances are made up of hundreds or even thousands of atoms. These really big molecules are called giant molecules or macromolecules.

Organic molecules

Many compounds with huge, complex molecules, such as proteins, are found in the cells of animals and plants. They are called **organic compounds**. All organic compounds contain the element carbon. Carbon atoms can form four bonds. They join with each other to form long chains, often with branches, and sometimes complete rings of atoms. Organic compounds are also found in crude oil, gas, and coal because these were formed from the remains of animals and plants.

Polymers

A polymer is an organic compound with extremely long chains made up of thousands of carbon atoms. Polymers are made by joining hundreds or thousands of smaller molecules (called monomers) together. This process is called polymerization.

◀ A model of a molecule of butane (C_4H_{10}). Butane is an organic compound with a chain of four carbon atoms.

All plastics are polymers. One example is the plastic polythene. Polythene is made by joining up ethene molecules. It is used to make items such as plastic sheets and milk jugs.

The amazing buckyball

Some organic compounds have molecules that are like cages of carbon atoms. These molecules are called fullerenes, and they can be shaped like balls or cylinders. One of the first to be discovered was made up of 60 carbon atoms. It was called buckminsterfullerene (nicknamed the buckyball) after the American architect Buckminster Fuller. He invented a similar-shaped dome for buildings. Buckyballs and buckytubes (or nanotubes) are already used to make high-resistance coatings, electronic components, water filters, and ultra-strong materials. Potentially, they have hundreds more applications.

DISCOVERING DNA

The chemical **DNA** is present in every cell of animals and plants. It contains the **genes** that pass **genetic information** from one generation to the next. A molecule of DNA is very complicated, and it contains more than a billion atoms. At the beginning of the 1950s, scientists knew that DNA existed but they did not know the structure of its molecule. In 1951 the British scientist Rosalind Franklin (1920–1958) analyzed DNA using a technique called X-ray crystallography. This showed that DNA has a structure like a twisted ladder. British scientist Francis Crick and American scientist James Watson used this information to help them build a model of DNA. This was one of the most important steps in the development of the science of genetics. DNA is short for deoxyribonucleic acid.

Forming solids

Substances come in three different forms or states—solids, liquids, and gases. A solid is a substance that keeps its shape and does not flow like a gas or a liquid. Most elements and compounds are solids at room temperature. Inside solids, the particles (which are either atoms, ions, or molecules) are packed tightly together and joined to their neighbors—but what holds a solid together? The answer is the bonds between the particles that make it up.

Different properties

Many of the properties of a substance, such as its strength and its melting and boiling points, depend on how its particles are arranged and what sort of bond joins them together.

If the bonds between the particles in a substance are very strong, the substance will have a high melting point and boiling point. This means that it will be a solid at room temperature. For example, sodium chloride (common salt) melts at 801 °C (1,474 °F), so it is a solid at room temperature. It is made of sodium ions and chloride ions joined together by **ionic bonds**. Ionic bonds are very strong, so **ionic compounds** such as sodium chloride have very high melting points and boiling points. Giant molecules are also solids at room temperature. For example, diamond melts at over 3,550 °C (6,422 °F)! In diamond, each carbon atom is joined to four other carbon atoms by covalent bonds. Covalent bonds are very strong, and diamond has many of them, so it has a very high melting point and boiling point.

If the bonds between the particles in a substance are weak, the substance will have a low melting point and boiling point. This means that it will be a liquid or a gas at room temperature. For example, at room temperature, water is a liquid and carbon dioxide is a gas. This is because they are made of simple molecules. There are strong covalent bonds between the atoms in a simple molecule, but the bonds between the molecules are weak and easily broken.

The particles in quartz crystals have strong bonds between them.

EXPERIMENT: DIAMOND AND GRAPHITE

Problem Diamond and graphite are two forms of the same element—carbon. Why are their properties so different?

EQUIPMENT
- modeling clay
- matchsticks or wooden dowels

Hypothesis Diamond and graphite are both made up of only carbon atoms. The differences between them may be because the carbon atoms are joined in different arrangements.

Experiment steps

1 Make 20 balls about ½ inch (10 millimeters) across from modeling clay. These are model carbon atoms.
2 Make a model of a piece of diamond like the one shown in this picture (right). Each carbon atom is attached to four others around it to make a three-dimensional structure.

3 Make a model of a piece of graphite as shown (left). Each carbon atom is attached to three others like a honeycomb to make sheets. Each sheet is loosely attached to one sheet above and one below.

Results

You can see that the structure of diamond is very strong because the atoms cannot move around in the structure. Graphite is made up of sheets of carbon atoms which can slide past each other, so it is not as strong.

27

THE PARTICLE MODEL

We can explain many of the properties and behavior of substances by thinking of them as being made up of tiny particles that are atoms, ions, or molecules. This model of substances is known as the particle model. The particle model helps explain the differences between solids, liquids, and gases, and what happens during melting and boiling.

Solids, liquids, and gases

The particles in solids, liquids, and gases are arranged differently and can move differently. In solids, the particles are close together and arranged neatly in a regular pattern. The bonds between the particles hold them tightly in place, so the particles in a solid can only vibrate where they are. They cannot move about or change places with their neighbors. This means that solids keep their shape and cannot flow.

In liquids, the particles are close together, but they are not arranged neatly in a regular pattern. The bonds between the particles hold them tightly, but they can break and then form again. This allows the particles in a liquid to move around each other. This means that liquids can flow into the bottom of any container they are in.

In gases, the particles are widely spaced, and they are not arranged neatly in a regular pattern. There are no bonds between the particles, so the particles can zoom around randomly at high speed. This means that gases can flow to completely fill any container they are in.

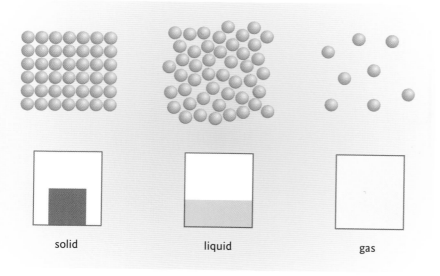

solid   liquid   gas

◀ Solids cannot flow, because there are strong bonds between the particles. A liquid flows to the bottom of a container, while a gas flows to fill it.

EXPERIMENT: PARTICLES IN SOLIDS, LIQUIDS, AND GASES

Problem Why do solids, liquids, and gases flow differently?

Hypothesis Solids, liquids, and gases flow differently because of how the particles that make them up are joined. We can use model particles to test this.

EQUIPMENT
- modeling clay
- glass jar with lid

Experiment steps

1 Use the modeling clay to make 12 to 15 small balls, each about ¼ inch (10 millimeters) across. Place them in a glass jar and put the lid on.

2 Tip and roll the jar gently in your hand (below) and watch what happens to the balls.

3 Now shake the jar as you roll it around and watch what happens.

4 Finally, shake the jar really hard and watch what happens.

Results

In step 2 the balls stick to each other, they do not flow at all, but make a solid. In step 3 the balls stick a little, but flow into the bottom of the jar, and make a liquid. In step 4 the balls do not stick at all, they flow all over the jar. They make a gas.

Gas pressure

When a gas is put into a container, the particles of gas zoom about hitting each other and the sides of the container. The particles of gas are very small because they are usually single atoms or simple molecules. However, there are millions upon millions of them in a cupful of gas, so many of them are hitting the inside of the container all the time. This means that the gas particles push against the surface of the container. This push is called gas pressure.

Diffusion

When different liquids or gases are put into the same container, they gradually mix even if they are not stirred. This mixing is called **diffusion**. Diffusion happens because the particles in liquids and gases can move around, and so they gradually spread into each other. This is how smells reach your nose through the air, even when there is no breeze blowing. For example, if a bottle of perfume is opened, particles from the perfume move quickly, mixing with the particles in the air, and reaching your nose by diffusion.

When you squeeze a bicycle pump, the air molecules inside are pushed together, making the pressure rise. They hit the end of the piston more often, pushing it outwards.

EXPERIMENT: DIFFUSION OF LIQUIDS

Problem

How can we show that diffusion happens in liquids?

Hypothesis

By putting colored liquids next to each other, we can see if they mix together without any mechanical mixing.

EQUIPMENT
- two identical glass jars
- aluminum foil
- Vaseline
- food coloring

Experiment steps

1 Smear the rim of one of the jars with Vaseline, then fill the jar to the brim with warm water. Add a few drops of food coloring to the water.

2 Cut a piece of aluminum foil that will fit over the mouth of the jar, and smooth the foil over the mouth and down over the neck. It does not matter if some air is trapped under the foil.

3 Do these next steps over a sink in case it goes wrong! Smear the rim of the other jar with Vaseline and fill to the brim with warm water. Overfill so that the jar is really full. Take the jar with the colored water and turn it upside down over the jar with the colorless water.

4 Wait a few minutes for the water to settle. You might need a helper to hold the bottom jar firmly. Hold onto the top jar and very slowly pull the foil out. You must keep the rims of the two jars exactly together while you do this. Watch what happens over the next few minutes.

Results

What happens to the water in the two jars? What do you think this means is happening to the particles of water in each jar? You can check your results on page 47.

Heating and cooling

The **particle** theory helps explain what happens to substances when they are heated up or cooled down. It explains why substances expand (get bigger) when they are heated, and why they melt or boil. It also explains why substances contract (get smaller) when they are cooled down, and why they freeze or **condense**.

Expansion and contraction

In a solid, the particles cannot move around because they are joined tightly to each other, but they can vibrate where they are. As a solid is heated up, its particles get more energy and they vibrate more and more. The higher the temperature, the more the particles vibrate. The particles do not get bigger, but they do take up more space, and this makes the solid expand slightly. Liquids also expand as their particles move more quickly.

When a gas is heated up, its particles move faster and faster. This means that the particles hit the sides of the container that the gas is in faster and more often. So the pressure that the gas exerts on the container is greater. If there is no container, the gas expands to fill more space.

Metal rails expand in hot weather. Expansion joints allow this to happen, without the rails buckling.

EXPANDING METALS

1 The apparatus (right) has two parts: a metal rod and holder. When the rod is cold it just fits inside the holder.

2 If the metal rod is heated by a Bunsen burner, it expands slightly and becomes too big to fit inside the holder.

EXPERIMENT: EXPANDING AIR

Problem

How can we show that air expands when it is heated?

Hypothesis

Gases expand much more than solids when they are heated. We can detect the air expanding and escaping from a bottle as it warms up.

EQUIPMENT
- empty plastic bottle
- small coin

Experiment steps

1 Wet a coin and rest it over the top of an empty plastic pop bottle. Put your hands around the bottle without squeezing it. Watch the coin carefully.

Results

Wait and watch for a few seconds. What happens to the coin? What do you think is happening to the air inside the bottle? You can check your results on page 47.

Temperature and heat

The particle model also helps to explain temperature and heat, and the difference between them. The temperature of an object is a measure of how hot it is. The more the particles in an object are vibrating, the higher its temperature.

Heat is a form of energy. When an object is heated, each particle gets more energy and vibrates more, and the object's temperature rises. A large metal block has more particles than a smaller block. If you add the same amount of heat to each block, the smaller one will become hotter than the larger one. This is because each particle gets more heat energy and vibrates more.

Changes of state

The particle theory explains how substances change from solid to liquid, and from liquid to gas. These changes are called changes of state, and they happen when the chemical bonds between particles break. When a solid is heated, its particles vibrate more and more until some of the bonds between them break. This allows the particles to begin moving around each other, and the substance becomes a liquid. When a solid turns into a liquid, it is called melting.

In a pan of boiling water the particles, which are water molecules, are breaking away from each other to form a gas, which we call steam.

When a liquid is heated, its particles move faster and faster. The bonds to some of the particles break completely. These particles can escape from the liquid to form a gas. When a liquid turns into a gas in this way, it is called boiling. Liquids can also turn into gases by evaporating. This happens when some particles in the liquid already have enough energy to escape to form a gas. Evaporating happens at temperatures below the boiling point of the liquid.

The particle theory also shows how substances change from gas to liquid, and from liquid to solid. These changes of state happen when bonds between particles are made. When a gas is cooled, its particles slow down until some bonds begin to form between the particles, and the particles join together to form a liquid. This is called condensing. When a liquid is cooled, its particles slow down so much that many bonds form. The particles join up in a regular pattern to make a solid. This is called freezing or solidifying.

Making solutions

A **solution** is made when a solid dissolves in a liquid. For example, if you put common salt in water, the salt crystals get smaller and seem to disappear as they dissolve. The particles on the outside of the crystal are pulled off by the water molecules, as the water molecules collide with the crystals. They then diffuse through the water. The hotter the water, the faster the water molecules move and the faster the salt dissolves.

Sunshine has heated the water in this lake, making it evaporate into the air. Evaporation happens faster when the temperature is higher and the air is dry.

SPLITTING ATOMS

When atoms take part in chemical reactions they can lose some electrons or gain some electrons, but the particles in their nuclei stay together. However, the nucleus of an atom can be split up, or have extra neutrons and protons added to it. When this happens it is called a nuclear reaction, because the nucleus changes.

Nuclear reactions can be both harmful and helpful. For example, the radiation they release can cause cancer, but in small doses radiation is actually used to kill cancer cells. Also, the energy the reactions release can create giant, destructive explosions, but it is also used to produce electricity.

Radioactive elements

The atoms of some elements, such as uranium, have nuclei that contain hundreds of protons and neutrons. Nuclei this big are quite unstable, and neutrons and protons often break away—making the nuclei smaller and more stable. This process is called **radioactive decay**, and the atoms that decay are radioactive. After a nuclear reaction, the nucleus of an atom often has fewer protons than it did before—so the atom has become an atom of a different element.

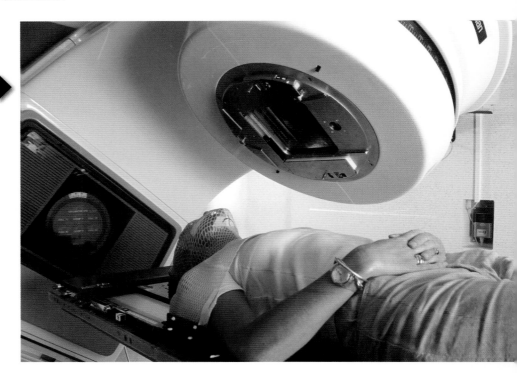

Radiotherapy is the use of radiation in medicine to try to kill cancer cells. Here a patient is receiving treatment for a brain tumor. Her head is being held in place by plastic webbing.

Here's an example of a nuclear reaction. Uranium has an atomic number of 92, so all uranium atoms contain 92 protons. Some uranium atoms contain 146 neutrons, which means they have a mass number of 238. This form of uranium is called uranium-238. When the nucleus of a uranium-238 atom decays, it loses a particle, called an alpha particle, which is made up of two protons and two neutrons. This leaves the nucleus with 90 protons and 144 neutrons. The atom's atomic number has changed, so it is no longer an atom of uranium. It is now an atom of an element called thorium.

Radiation

When a nucleus breaks up, it releases radiation. Radiation can be made up of particles, such as the alpha particles mentioned above. Radiation can also be made up of rays. These rays are like light rays, but they are invisible and have so much more energy that they can go through solid sheets of metal. Strong radiation causes radiation sickness, which makes people feel sick and be sick. It can also cause burns to skin, and cancers. Radioactive substances are stored in lead-lined boxes that keeps radiation from escaping.

Natural radiation

Most rocks contain radioactive elements, so there is always a small, harmless amount of natural radiation from the ground. This is called background radiation. All living things contain millions of carbon atoms, some of which are called carbon-14 atoms because they contain two more neutrons than a normal carbon atom. These atoms decay naturally so even your body creates tiny amounts of radiation!

This hazard symbol warns that there are high levels of harmful radiation in the area.

Nuclear energy

In radioactive decay, neutrons and protons split from the nucleus of an atom, leaving a slightly smaller nucleus behind. Nuclei can also split in two, to make two smaller nuclei. This sort of nuclear reaction is also called nuclear fission. It means that an atom of one element becomes two atoms of different elements.

Nuclear fission happens naturally, but we can also make it happen deliberately by firing sub-atomic particles such as neutrons into a large nucleus. For example, when a neutron is fired into the nucleus of an atom of uranium-235, the atom splits into an atom of an element called strontium and an atom of an element called xenon. Some neutrons are also released. If there are more atoms of uranium nearby, these freed neutrons make them split up, too, and these also release neutrons, and so on. This is called a chain reaction. Nuclear fission also produces a large amount of heat energy, which is called nuclear energy.

Nuclear power

In a nuclear power station, the energy from nuclear fission is turned into electrical energy for use in factories, offices, and homes. The reaction happens in a chamber called a nuclear reactor. Inside the reactor a chain reaction happens, but its speed is carefully controlled. The reaction produces a staggering amount of energy—just three hundredths of an ounce of uranium fuel creates enough energy to run a light bulb continuously for 20 years!

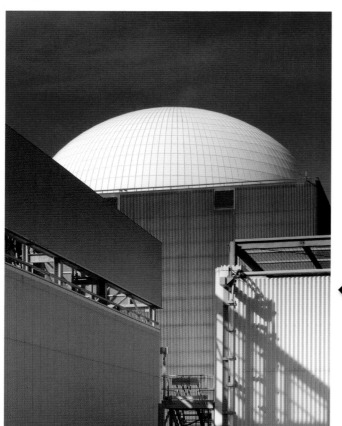

Sizewell B nuclear power station in England. The nuclear reactor is inside the domed building in the center.

Nuclear waste

Nuclear energy seems to be a good alternative to burning fossil fuels for producing energy, but it does create problems. The used fuel from nuclear power stations stays radioactive for thousands of years, so it has to be buried in concrete bunkers deep underground. Radioactive chemicals have also leaked from chemical plants into the seas and the atmosphere, where radiation from it may harm wildlife and people.

Nuclear fusion

Nuclear fusion is the opposite of nuclear fission. It is a nuclear reaction in which two nuclei join together to form a larger nucleus. Like fission, fusion releases large amounts of energy. It is nuclear fusion that happens inside the Sun.

ACCIDENT AT CHERNOBYL

The worst accident in the history of nuclear power happened at the Chernobyl nuclear power station in the Ukraine in 1986. The station's operators made several mistakes that allowed the reactor to run out of control, and 32 people were killed in the explosions and fires that followed. The radioactive substances that leaked from the reactor were carried across Europe by the wind, and people and animals later died from radiation sickness. Thousands more may die because of the radiation they received during and after the accident.

THE PERIODIC TABLE

The periodic table is a chart of all the known elements. The elements are arranged in order of their atomic numbers, but in rows, so that elements with similar properties are underneath each other. The periodic table gets its name from the fact that the elements' properties repeat themselves every few elements, or periodically. The position of an element in the periodic table gives an idea of what its properties are likely to be.

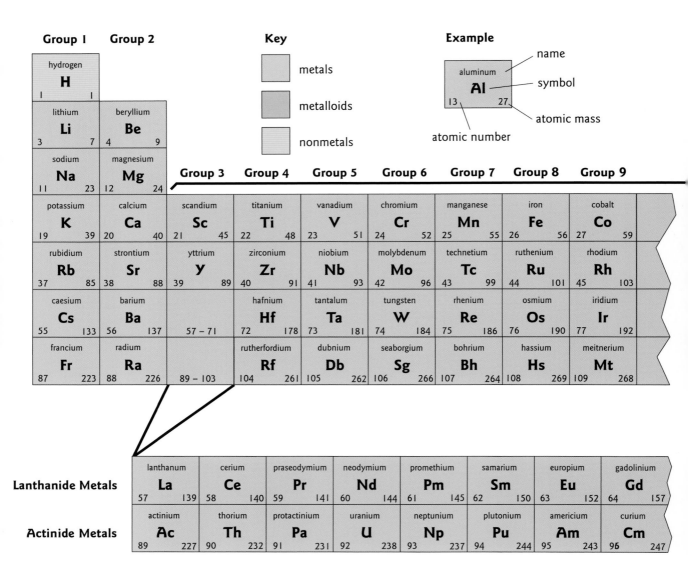

Key

- metals
- metalloids
- nonmetals

Example

	aluminum — name
	Al — symbol
13	27 — atomic mass
atomic number	

Group 1	Group 2	Group 3	Group 4	Group 5	Group 6	Group 7	Group 8	Group 9
hydrogen **H** 1 · 1								
lithium **Li** 3 · 7	beryllium **Be** 4 · 9							
sodium **Na** 11 · 23	magnesium **Mg** 12 · 24							
potassium **K** 19 · 39	calcium **Ca** 20 · 40	scandium **Sc** 21 · 45	titanium **Ti** 22 · 48	vanadium **V** 23 · 51	chromium **Cr** 24 · 52	manganese **Mn** 25 · 55	iron **Fe** 26 · 56	cobalt **Co** 27 · 59
rubidium **Rb** 37 · 85	strontium **Sr** 38 · 88	yttrium **Y** 39 · 89	zirconium **Zr** 40 · 91	niobium **Nb** 41 · 93	molybdenum **Mo** 42 · 96	technetium **Tc** 43 · 99	ruthenium **Ru** 44 · 101	rhodium **Rh** 45 · 103
caesium **Cs** 55 · 133	barium **Ba** 56 · 137	57 – 71	hafnium **Hf** 72 · 178	tantalum **Ta** 73 · 181	tungsten **W** 74 · 184	rhenium **Re** 75 · 186	osmium **Os** 76 · 190	iridium **Ir** 77 · 192
francium **Fr** 87 · 223	radium **Ra** 88 · 226	89 – 103	rutherfordium **Rf** 104 · 261	dubnium **Db** 105 · 262	seaborgium **Sg** 106 · 266	bohrium **Bh** 107 · 264	hassium **Hs** 108 · 269	meitnerium **Mt** 109 · 268

Lanthanide Metals

lanthanum **La** 57 · 139	cerium **Ce** 58 · 140	praseodymium **Pr** 59 · 141	neodymium **Nd** 60 · 144	promethium **Pm** 61 · 145	samarium **Sm** 62 · 150	europium **Eu** 63 · 152	gadolinium **Gd** 64 · 157

Actinide Metals

actinium **Ac** 89 · 227	thorium **Th** 90 · 232	protactinium **Pa** 91 · 231	uranium **U** 92 · 238	neptunium **Np** 93 · 237	plutonium **Pu** 94 · 244	americium **Am** 95 · 243	curium **Cm** 96 · 247

Groups and periods

The vertical columns of elements are called groups. The horizontal rows of elements are called periods. Some groups have special names:

Group 1: Alkali metals
Group 2: Alkaline earth metals
Groups 3–12: Transition metals
Group 17: Halogens
Group 18: Noble gases

The table is divided into two main sections, the metals and nonmetals. Between the two are elements that have some properties of metals and some of nonmetals. They are called semimetals or **metalloids**.

			Group 13	Group 14	Group 15	Group 16	Group 17	Group 18
								helium **He** 2 · 4
			boron **B** 5 · 11	carbon **C** 6 · 12	nitrogen **N** 7 · 14	oxygen **O** 8 · 16	fluorine **F** 9 · 19	neon **Ne** 10 · 20
Group 10	Group 11	Group 12	aluminum **Al** 13 · 27	silicon **Si** 14 · 28	phosphorus **P** 15 · 31	sulfur **S** 16 · 32	chlorine **Cl** 17 · 35	argon **Ar** 18 · 40
nickel **Ni** 28 · 59	copper **Cu** 29 · 64	zinc **Zn** 30 · 65	gallium **Ga** 31 · 70	germanium **Ge** 32 · 73	arsenic **As** 33 · 75	selenium **Se** 34 · 79	bromine **Br** 35 · 80	krypton **Kr** 36 · 84
palladium **Pd** 46 · 106	silver **Ag** 47 · 108	cadmium **Cd** 48 · 112	indium **In** 49 · 115	tin **Sn** 50 · 119	antimony **Sb** 51 · 122	tellurium **Te** 52 · 128	iodine **I** 53 · 127	xenon **Xe** 54 · 131
platinum **Pt** 78 · 195	gold **Au** 79 · 197	mercury **Hg** 80 · 201	thallium **Tl** 81 · 204	lead **Pb** 82 · 207	bismuth **Bi** 83 · 209	polonium **Po** 84 · 209	astatine **At** 85 · 210	radon **Rn** 86 · 222
darmstadtium **Ds** 110 · 281	roentgenium **Rg** 111 · 272	ununbium **Uub** 112 · 285	ununtrium **Uut** 113 · 284	ununquadium **Uuq** 114 · 289	ununpentium **Uup** 115 · 288	ununhexium **Uuh** 116 · 292		

terbium **Tb** 65 · 159	dysprosium **Dy** 66 · 163	holmium **Ho** 67 · 165	erbium **Er** 68 · 167	thulium **Tm** 69 · 169	ytterbium **Yb** 70 · 173	lutetium **Lu** 71 · 175
berkelium **Bk** 97 · 247	californium **Cf** 98 · 251	einsteinium **Es** 99 · 252	fermium **Fm** 100 · 257	mendelevium **Md** 101 · 258	nobelium **No** 102 · 259	lawrencium **Lr** 103 · 262

Common elements

Here is a table of the most common elements from the periodic table that you may find at home or in your school's science classroom. The table gives the atomic mass (the total number of protons and neutrons in the nucleus of an atom of the element), indicates whether it is a solid, liquid, or gas at room temperature, and shows how the atoms join together in a piece of the element.

Element	Symbol	Atomic mass	State at room temperature	Structure	Formula
hydrogen	H	1	gas	molecules	H_2
helium	He	4	gas	single atoms	He
lithium	Li	7	solid	metallic	
carbon	C	12	solid	giant molecules	
nitrogen	N	14	gas	molecules	N_2
oxygen	O	16	gas	molecules	O_2
fluorine	F	19	gas	molecules	F_2
neon	Ne	20	gas	single atoms	Ne
sodium	Na	23	solid	metallic	
magnesium	Mg	24	solid	metallic	
aluminum	Al	27	solid	metallic	
silicon	Si	28	solid	giant molecules	
phosphorus	P	31	solid	molecules	P_4
sulfur	S	32	solid	molecules	S_8
chlorine	Cl	35	gas	molecules	Cl_2
argon	Ar	40	gas	single atoms	Ar
potassium	K	39	solid	metallic	
calcium	Ca	40	solid	metallic	
iron	Fe	56	solid	metallic	
copper	Cu	64	solid	metallic	
zinc	Zn	65	solid	metallic	
bromine	Br	80	liquid	molecules	Br_2
silver	Ag	108	solid	metallic	
tin	Sn	119	solid	metallic	
iodine	I	127	solid	molecules	I_2
gold	Au	197	solid	metallic	
mercury	Hg	201	liquid	metallic	
lead	Pb	207	solid	metallic	

Common compounds

Here is a table of some common compounds, made up of two or more elements, that you may find at home or in your school's science classroom. The middle column tells you what the particles of the compound are like.

Compound	Structure	Formula
Gases		
carbon dioxide	molecules	CO_2
carbon monoxide	molecules	CO
nitrogen dioxide	molecules	NO_2
methane	molecules	CH_4
Liquids and solutions		
water	molecules	H_2O
hydrochloric acid	ions in solution	HCl
sulfuric acid	ions in solution	H_2SO_4
nitric acid	ions in solution	HNO_3
sodium hydroxide	ions in solution	$NaOH$
Solids		
sodium chloride	ionic	$NaCl$
magnesium oxide	ionic	MgO
calcium carbonate	ionic	$CaCO_3$
copper sulfate	ionic	$CuSO_4$

SEE ORIGINAL ROW BELOW

Atoms and shells

This table shows the number of protons, neutrons, and electrons in the atoms of some elements as well as their atomic mass (W). It also shows how the electrons are arranged in shells. The first shell can hold 8 atoms at most, the second 8, and the third 18. The fourth shell begins to fill before the third is full.

Element	Symbol	Protons	Neutrons	Atomic Mass	Electrons	Shells
hydrogen	H	1	0	1	1	1
helium	He	2	2	4	2	2
lithium	Li	3	4	7	3	2, 1
carbon	C	6	6	12	6	2, 4
oxygen	O	8	8	16	8	2, 6
neon	Ne	10	10	20	10	2, 8
sodium	Na	11	12	23	11	2, 8, 1
magnesium	Mg	12	12	24	12	2, 8, 2
aluminum	Al	13	14	27	13	2, 8, 3
silicon	Si	14	14	28	14	2, 8, 4
chlorine	Cl	17	18	35	17	2, 8, 7
argon	Ar	18	22	40	18	2, 8, 8
potassium	K	19	20	39	19	2, 8, 8, 1
calcium	Ca	20	20	40	20	2, 8, 8, 1

These diagrams show examples of arrangements of electrons.

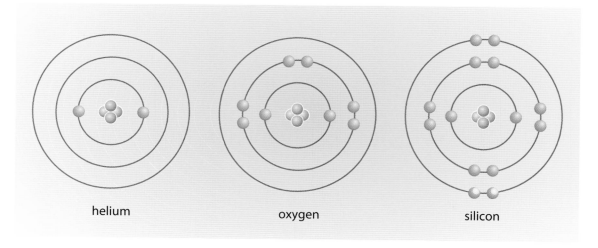

helium   oxygen   silicon

GLOSSARY OF TECHNICAL TERMS

atmosphere thick blanket of air that surrounds Earth

atom extremely tiny particle of matter. An atom is the smallest particle of an element that can exist. All substances are made up of atoms.

atomic theory theory that all substances are made up of a limited number of types of atom combined together in different ways

boiling point temperature at which a substance changes state from liquid to gas

chain reaction series of nuclear reactions in which the particles emitted from one nucleus set off a reaction in another nucleus

charge electricity on an object, such as an atom or electron

chemical bond force that binds atoms, ions, or molecules together

chemical formulas collection of symbols and numbers that represents an element or compound. It shows what elements are in a compound and the ratio of the numbers of atoms of each element.

compound substance that contains two or more different elements joined together by chemical bonds

condense turn from a gas to a liquid

conduct to let electricity or heat pass through a substance, called a conductor

covalent bond chemical bond formed when two atoms share one or more electrons

decay when the nucleus of an atom gradually becomes smaller and lighter as particles are ejected from it in nuclear reactions

diffusion random movement of the particles through a liquid or a gas

DNA very complex chemical in every living cell that carries the genetic information for the animal or plant

electron extremely tiny particle that is part of an atom. Electrons move around the nucleus of an atom.

element substance that contains just one type of atom. Elements are the simplest substances that exist.

fossil fuel natural fuel such as coal or gas, formed over thousands of years from the remains of living things

gene section of DNA that carries the code for making a protein. Genes are passed from one generation to the next.

genetic information information contained in genes as a complex chemical code. It controls how living cells are made and what they do.

ion type of particle. An ion is an atom that has lost or gained one or more electrons, giving it an overall positive or negative charge.

ionic bond chemical bond between two ions with opposite charges that attract each other

ionic compound compound made up of ions of two different elements

matter stuff that everything in the Universe is made from. There are three states of matter: solids, liquids, and gases.

melting point temperature at which a substance changes state from solid to liquid as it warms

metal any element in the periodic table that is shiny, and that conducts electricity and heat well. Most metals are also hard.

metalloid element that cannot be classed as a metal or a nonmetal. It has some of the properties of a metal and some of the properties of a nonmetal.

mixture substance made up of two or more elements or compounds that are not joined together by chemical bonds

molecule type of particle. A molecule is made up of two or more atoms joined together by chemical bonds. The atoms can be of the same element or different elements.

neutron one of the particles that makes up the nucleus of an atom

nonmetal any element in the periodic table that is not a metal. Most nonmetals are gases.

nuclear fission nuclear reaction in which the nucleus of an atom splits into two parts

nucleus (nuclei) central part of an atom, made up of protons and neutrons

organic compound compounds found in living things, or in the remains of living things

particle small piece of a substance, such as an atom, ion, or molecule

polymer compound that has molecules made up of lots of small molecules that are all the same, joined together in a long chain

properties characteristics of a substance, such as its strength, melting point, and density

proton one of the particles that makes up the nucleus of an atom

radiation rays, such as light and heat, or streams of particles. Exposure to large amounts of radiation can be extremely harmful to people, animals, and the environment.

radioactive substance that gives off radiation

reactive chemical that takes part in chemical reactions easily

shells layers of electrons around the nucleus of an atom

solution substance made when a solid, gas, or liquid dissolves in a liquid. The substance that dissolves is called the solute and the liquid it dissolves in is called the solvent.

sub-atomic particle particle that is part of an atom. Protons, neutrons, and electrons are sub-atomic particles.

symbol single letter or two letters used to represent an element in chemical formulas and equations

theories ideas about how something, for example science, works

X-ray form of radiation that passes through flesh but is stopped by bones

FURTHER READING

Clowes, Martin and Woodford, Chris. *Atoms and Molecules.* Farmington Hills, Mich.: Blackbirch Press, 2004.

e. science encyclopedia. New York: DK Publishing, 2004.

Parsons, Jayne. *The Way Science Works.* New York: DK Publishing, 2002.

Solway, Andrew. *A History of Super Science: Atoms and Elements.* Chicago: Raintree-Heinemann, 2006.

Useful websites

http://www.billnye.com
Includes a number of physical science experiements to do at home.

http://www.chem4kids.com
A lot of information and activities on chemistry, presented in a fun way.

http://www.chemicalelements.com
An interactive Periodic table. Originally created, in 1996, as an 8th grade science project.

http://www.creative-chemistry.org.uk
An interactive chemistry site including fun practical activities, worksheets, quizzes, puzzles, and more!

http://www.heinemannexplore.com
An online resource for school libraries and classrooms containing articles, investigations, biographies, and activities related to all areas of the science curriculum.

http://www.webelements.com/ webelements/scholar
The Periodic table – online! Discover more about all the elements and their properties.

Experiment results

page 31: The color spreads from one jar to the other. This shows that the particles of water from both jars are diffusing into each other.

page 33: After a few seconds, the coin moves slightly. This is because the heat from your hands has caused the air in the bottle to expand. The air no longer fits inside the bottle, so the coin is pushed aside to allow the air to escape

INDEX